Amazing St...ies From G...

...of Nature

WILD
'n'
Wacky

Amazing Stories From God's World of Nature

WILD 'n' Wacky

Ray Montgomery

REVIEW AND HERALD® PUBLISHING ASSOCIATION
HAGERSTOWN, MD 21740

The author assumes full responsibility for the accuracy of all facts and
quotations as cited in this book.

Bible texts are from the *Holy Bible, New International Version.* Copyright ©
1973, 1978, 1984, Internatonal Bible Society. Used by permission of
Zondervan Bible Publishers.

This book was
Edited by Randy Fishell
Cover/interior design by Trent Truman
Cover illustration by Extraordinair Art Inc./Gary Fasen
Electronic makeup by Shirley M. Bolivar
Typeset: 13/16 Berkeley Book

PRINTED IN U.S.A.

05 04 03 02 01   5 4 3 2 1

R&H Cataloging Service
Montgomery, Ray N., 1903-1995
    Wild 'n' wacky: amazing stories from God's wonderful world of nature.

    1. Natural history—Miscellanea.   I. Title.

                        508

ISBN 0-8280-1507-4

Dedication

This
book is
dedicated to

Irene Carney Montgomery,

Virginia Shockley Montgomery,
Thornton W. Burgess,

and

Promise Kloss Sherman Moffett.

contents

Chapter One

BIG AND LITTLE BEASTIES

DON'T BE AFRAID—IT'S JUST A LION

People usually picture the African lion as "lord of the jungle" or "king of the beasts." But according to professionals who have studied the lion closely, his "crown" has slipped a bit. The lion isn't as brave and fierce as we've been led to believe. A single hyena has been known to defeat him, and a shout from a human being can turn his fierceness into retreat. (It can be a different story if the lion is really hungry, however!)

There have been instances when the combined yells of several people have caused man-eaters, such as lions and tigers, to slink away. Africans sometimes resort to shouting to keep hippos, elephants, and wild pigs out of their crops at night, and a sudden loud yell has been known to stop a charging rhino. The words of God, recorded in Genesis 9:2, are truer than you may have realized: "The fear and dread of you will fall upon all the beasts of the earth and all the birds of the air, upon every creature that moves along the ground, and upon all the fish of the sea."

THE BEAST WITH A 17-POUND BRAIN

Facts prove that it is actually the elephant who should be crowned king of beasts. Ten times larger than the lion, he is wiser, useful, and usually peaceful. The African pachyderm (a Greek word meaning thick-skinned), or elephant, is the mightiest of all land animals, with an average height of 10 feet 6 inches, and a weight of from 12,000 to 16,000 pounds. He has a 17-pound brain and can crush a lion with one foot. The tusks, that are actually teeth, are often 10 feet long. The African elephant has the largest ears of any animal on earth. Since it is a ruminant, that is, it eats and chews grass, its teeth wear out quickly. To remedy this, a wise Creator has given the elephant the ability to grow new teeth. During its lifetime of from 60 to 130 years, six sets of teeth are possible. Beside the elephant's stomach is a water reservoir that holds 10 gallons of refreshment.

DANGER IN THE JUNGLE

Elephants have been known to become man killers, or rogues. A rogue elephant in northern Zululand killed 12 people, laid a village in ruins, terrorized users of a busy road, and charged a railroad train. He became known as the Dabi killer. The beast's bad ways ended when a hunter, John Taylor, found him raiding a millet field.

W. Robert Foran, a famous big-game hunter, was

eLePHaNTS aRe a LoT LiKe WHO?

Elephants have many human-like characteristics, including extreme concern with the welfare of their young. One elephant mother saw her baby, who was well able to walk, wandering dangerously near the over-hanging bank of a river. She trumpeted her anxiety, but the baby paid no attention. Suddenly the bank gave way, plunging the youngster into deep water.

Immediately, several ele-phants hurried to the rescue. When the baby was back on solid ground, the mother felt him carefully with her trunk, assuring herself that he was not injured. Then she gave him a mighty whack with her trunk and sent him bawling on his way.

Another time an elephant calf died three days after birth, and for two days the grieving mother carried the still form on her tusks, show-ing signs of anger when ap-proached. On the third day she dug a shallow grave at the foot of a baobab tree and gently buried the body.

surprised along a jungle trail by a giant male elephant. Foran shot him in the chest. Before a second shot was possible, the animal twisted his trunk around the man and threw him bodily into a thorn tree. Badly bruised and shirtless, Foran disentangled himself and secured his rifle, which he had dropped as he fell into the tree. Though wounded, the elephant ran away.

What turns a normally passive animal into a rogue? One cause is nonfatal wounds inflicted by people trying to protect their crops or homes. Another cause is eating overripe, fermented marula fruit (the elephant, not you, silly). A drunken elephant is a terrifying engine of destruction. A third cause is infection at the root of a tusk that has been injured; the pain drives the elephant berserk.

The smallest men in Africa kill elephants by a

THE "BAD" SIDE OF NATURE

Have you ever wondered this: Did God create such creatures as rogue elephants, meat-eating animals, venomous snakes, and birds known as raptors?

Consider this first: Would a good and loving God create *anything* that would hurt or destroy any of His creatures? If not, who *is* responsible for meat-eating animals, raptors, poisonous plants, death-dealing insects, germs, and viruses? Here's one explanation that may help: "The same God who guides the planets works in the fruit orchard and in the vegetable garden. He never made a thorn, a thistle, or a tare. These are Satan's work, the result of degeneration [sin's effects], introduced by him among the precious things; but it is through God's immediate agency [presence and power], that every bud bursts into blossom" (*Testimonies*, vol. 6, p. 186).

Nature's occasional harshness is a complex matter, but the bottom line is that it's not God's ideal for His creation.

simple method. The Bushmen, or Pygmies, shoot them with arrows dipped in a poison known as curare, then follow patiently until the elephant collapses.

PACK YOUR TRUNK, SOLDIER

The first war elephants were trained in India thousands of years ago. They were mounts for spear throwers and carried wooden towers from which soldiers climbed walls. The Chinese began using war elephants around 2000 B.C. Some were actually trained to wield long swords with their trunks. Some were protected with metal armor. Just the sight of these giant animals charging foot soldiers, who had never seen an elephant, was enough to spread terror through the troops. In the Middle Ages, the king of Rangoon kept 500 war elephants. More recently, cannons were fired from their backs.

A Carthaginian army at Tunetum was led by a Macedonian general, Xanthippus. His army was larger than that of Atilius, having 4,000 horsemen, plus a surprise unit. As the two armies marched to meet in mortal combat, the Carthaginians began a surprising formation. Their ranks divided into three groups, leaving two open spaces between. Down these passages thundered war elephants in single file. The Roman soldiers had never seen anything like it. The mighty gray animals, wearing armor on their heads, shuffled rapidly forward. As they advanced, their trunks groping, the Romans fell back. Traveling at 15 miles an hour, the elephants were soon upon them, flailing, trumpeting, hurling soldiers into the air, trampling others under foot. The Carthaginian foot soldiers closed in behind them and cut down the demoralized survivors. Of the 15,000 Romans, a pitiful 500 men escaped.

COLD WAR CASUALTIES

After the Tunetum disaster, the Roman military recruited elephants for war. They were trained in either groups of 64, or phalanxes and "elephantarchies" of 16. Each warrior elephant was cared for by the handler and six soldiers.

Hannibal Barca (247-183 B.C.), a Carthaginian whose father, Hamilcar Barca, was ruler of Spain, was a bitter enemy of Rome. Upon the death of the older man, Hannibal set out to attack. With an army of 40,000 men and 38 elephants he determined to cross the Alps from France into Italy, but he was faced with a weighty problem: how to get the elephants over the Rhone River. Apparently, he either did not know elephants could swim or feared that the swollen waters would sweep them downstream. At any rate, his engineers constructed huge rafts to ferry the animals.

As the army approached the Alps, Hannibal employed several northern Italians who knew the Alpine passes and shared his hate for Rome. They guided him up through Col de Cabre, a passage requiring two weeks travel time. It was a disaster of sorts for elephants, men, and horses. Unfriendly Frenchmen rolled great stones down on them, and though it was early October, there was ice and snow in the higher passes. Elephants, horses, wagons, and men fell off the icy road to their deaths. Midway, a landslide stopped the advance. Hannibal had not considered the effect of cold on tropical animals, and the elephants that survived the icy road died of pneumonia. When the nightmare ended, Hannibal marched 26,000 soldiers and one lone elephant into northern Italy.

Hannibal's epic crossing of the Alps was recorded in detail by the Greek historian Polybius, who was a stickler for facts. To ensure the accuracy of his account, he traveled over the same route 60 years later. At that time the disjointed skeletons of Hannibal's elephants were still visible in ravines below the road.

Guide
FACTory
Facts about... ELEPHANTS

- Elephants require only one half the amount of sleep needed by humans. They are excellent swimmers and love water.

- An elephant requires 600 to 800 pounds of grass, leaves, twigs, or bark per day. In captivity they are fed 15 to 18 pounds of grain daily, along with 12 to 14 gallons of water.

▓ The elephant's trunk is a nose combined with the upper lip. It ends in a finger-like projection that contains the organs of smell, and is constructed of 40,000 muscles covered with a tough hide. This remarkable organ is so sensitive that it can pick up a pin, select a single blade of grass, uncork a bottle, untie a slip knot, unbolt a gate, throw—and catch—a baseball, ring a bell, sweep with a broom, or pick up a full-grown lion and throw it as far as 20 feet. (Can *you* do all that, never mind with your *nose?*)

▓ Elephants are often the prime attraction in circuses. The first circus elephant in the United States was brought to Boston in 1796 by a Yankee ship owner. In 1805 another elephant, named Old Bet, was imported by Mr. Hackaliath Bailey, of Somers, New York. Bet became the first circus elephant to go on tour. This event led to the founding of the original circus museum in that town.

▓ The first baby elephant to be born in the United States made her appearance in the Philadelphia zoo on March 10, 1880. She was promptly named Columbia and lived to be 25 years old. Newborn elephants weigh about 200 pounds. They are weaned in their fourth year.

▓ Asiatic elephants are smaller and more easily tamed and trained than African elephants. In India alone the population of work elephants numbers about 7,000.

HAVE YOU SEEN A SHREW?

The three-inch-long pigmy shrew, native to Maryland, Virginia, and North Carolina, is the tiniest mammalian vertebrate in North America. The two-inch, fat-tailed shrew, found in Europe, is the smallest mammalian vertebrate on *earth*.

The shrew has few enemies, and those that do catch it soon learn to avoid it, for it has a pouch that gives off a nauseating musk odor. This tornado of minuscule muscle is active 24 hours a day with time out for a brief catnap now and then. Its voracious appetite allows for no distinction between night and day.

The shrew is absolutely unafraid. The little critter is so savage that several leading naturalists have called it the fiercest animal for its size on earth. The expression, "runs like crazy," fits perfectly, for the animal's erratic racing seems without rhyme or reason as it darts here and there, burrowing in the earth or under leaves or grass in search of any kind of food. Its keen appetite is a result of its digestive system's rapid metabolism. A shrew needs at least its own weight in food daily. If it cannot obtain enough nourishment, it will starve to death in 24 hours. The animal is so high-strung that it often dies quickly when captured. The shrew is cursed with weak eyesight but blessed with a keen sense of smell. In order to survive, it must follow every clue its nose brings

HaPPY BIRTHDaY (now GeT OUT OF HeRe)

The tiny shrew is born in a grass-lined nest. An average litter consists of four to 10 bee-size young that are weaned in three weeks and are then fed mostly earthworms. Within four weeks they are out of the nest and, disowned by the fierce little mother, begin a fast-moving life that may last from 16 to 18 months.

WaTeR-SKIING WONDeR

The most amazing shrew of all is the walk-on-the-water species. A marsh-inhabiting animal, it frequents mountain lakes and streams. It is the largest of American shrews and is able to swim and dive as otters do. How can it walk on water? Well, it's a real lightweight, and its back feet are enlarged with hairs that imprison small air bubbles that act as pontoons. This shrew employs the scientific fact of surface tension and can water-ski with efficiency when it needs to. When swimming under water in search of insects, its fur is coated with a silvery layer of imprisoned air. To help it swim, our Creator has given this water-loving creature a vertically flattened tail, unlike the beaver's, which is horizontally flattened.

to it, animal or vegetable, dead or alive.

When facing an animal larger than itself, a shrew rears up on its hind feet, bares its teeth, and emits a high-pitched, chittering squeak. Then it hurries to the battle, where its fierceness enables it to kill rats, small snakes, moles, or another shrew.

FACTory Guide

Facts about... SHREWS

▨ Native Americans called the shrew "kin-skee-sha-wash-bee-gah-note-see," which means "short-tailed, sharp-nosed field mouse."

■ One squirrel-like variety lives in trees and acts much as squirrels do.

■ Relatively few people have ever seen a shrew, though they are plentiful worldwide. They are often mistaken for the common mole.

■ The shrew's value to humankind is the enormous number of insects it eats.

JUST HANGIN' AROUND

Monkeys, apes, chimpanzees, baboons, gibbons, gorillas, and orangutans are all known as primates, or simians.

The great apes are often depicted as maniacal killers, and the smaller apes as clowns. The picture of the gorilla as a huge mass of death-dealing muscle, beating its chest in a rage, is almost entirely false. Actually, it is a shy, human-avoiding creature whose furious display of ferociousness is 99 percent bluff.

HOW TO GET FRIENDS (THE HARD WAY)

Grooming is a social function among all simians. This often takes the form of searching through each other's hair for insects and dandruff-like flakes with a salty taste. In a zoo environment a close friendship may develop between a chimp and its keeper, and as evidence of this, the animal will roll up the keeper's shirt sleeve, carefully part nonexistent hair, and pick up and eat imaginary insects. This is simply to show friendship.

However, under certain conditions the gorilla can—
and will—kill. On the other hand, the long-lived primates establish a family relationship that endures for
life. They protect one another, share food, hold
hands, embrace, kiss, shake hands, and give each
other approving pats on the back. As for domestica-
tion, South African baboons have been trained to
herd sheep. In Borneo they regularly assist in har-
vesting coconuts.

GORILLA GENIUS

Just how intelligent are gorillas? Francine
Patterson, an animal psychologist, performed studies
on Koko, an 8-year-old female gorilla. Miss Patterson,
aware that previous investigators had determined that
primates could not communicate verbally, taught
Koko the American sign language, used by thousands
of deaf persons. The gorilla learned this method and
used it efficiently. It took one year to teach Koko 14
signs, but she eventually knew and used 375 signs.
Miss Patterson believed Koko's IQ was between 84
and 95, human scale.

Unfortunately, Koko knew how to argue, deceive,
and lie, among other things. She also knew when she
was misbehaving. Once, when she saw that her in-
structor was disturbed by her attitude, Koko signed,
"I'm a stubborn devil." When she had accidentally broken a kitchen fixture and was asked whether she had

done it, Koko shifted the blame to an assistant trainer and signed, "Kate did it." When asked whether she was an animal or a person, she signed, "Fine animal gorilla."

I'm Outta Here!

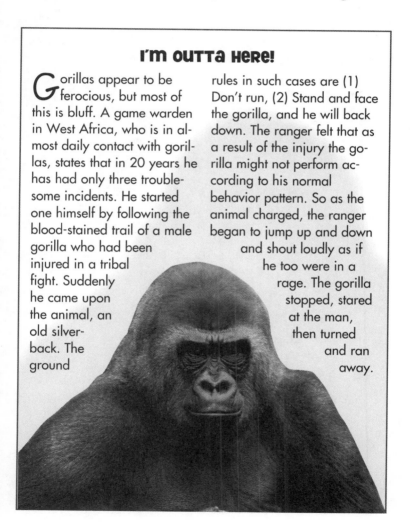

Gorillas appear to be ferocious, but most of this is bluff. A game warden in West Africa, who is in almost daily contact with gorillas, states that in 20 years he has had only three troublesome incidents. He started one himself by following the blood-stained trail of a male gorilla who had been injured in a tribal fight. Suddenly he came upon the animal, an old silverback. The ground rules in such cases are (1) Don't run, (2) Stand and face the gorilla, and he will back down. The ranger felt that as a result of the injury the gorilla might not perform according to his normal behavior pattern. So as the animal charged, the ranger began to jump up and down and shout loudly as if he too were in a rage. The gorilla stopped, stared at the man, then turned and ran away.

COOL CHIMPS

Chimpanzees are very adaptable. In experiments in Russia, five were isolated on an island. To observe the effect of cold on tropical animals, the experimenters allowed the enclosure temperature to drop to 40° Fahrenheit. The resourceful chimps constructed cozy hammock-like shelters of tree branches in which their body heat was utilized to the maximum. On their own, the chimps found 80 varieties of edible plants growing on the island.

Here's an insightful statement that brings Koko to mind: "The intelligence displayed by many dumb animals approaches so closely to human intelligence that it is a mystery. The animals see and hear and love and fear and suffer. They use their organs far more faithfully than many human beings use theirs. They manifest sympathy and tenderness toward their companions in suffering. Many animals show an affection for those who have charge of them, far superior to the affection shown by some of the human race. They form attachments for man which are not broken without great suffering to them" (*The Ministry of Healing,* pp. 315, 316).

BABOON GUARDS

Baboons live mostly on the ground. Since they

have no claws, they band together to repel enemies. Single baboons will sacrifice life for the protection of the family or troop, however. In one instance a troop slept in a cave on a cliff to which the only approach was a six-inch-wide path. One evening as the troop marched single file to the den, a leopard followed them. Two baboons moved out of line and went back

No Microphone Needed

In America there is a strange monkey called the alouatte, or howler monkey. It is the largest monkey in the New World. This native of Central and South America has red or black hair and an enlarged hyoid bone, located at the base of the tongue and at the opening into the windpipe, that gives a peculiar resonance to the voice. The call of this monkey can be heard as far as eight miles away. The sound is similar to a donkey's bray, combined with the bark of a dog. The alouattes spend considerable time howling in concert and, like the coyote, will serenade the moon.

In the Malay Peninsula the siamang gibbon has a different voice amplifier—an inflatable sac under the chin. These are the largest of all gibbons, and the inflated pouch gives their voice the resonance of a drum. The sound is a mixture of barks and whoops and can be heard a mile away.

Of all the monkeys, the most unusual are the lorisiform femurs of Africa. Their actions are completely opposite those of all other monkeys, which are alert, quick, and active. They move slowly and deliberately, as if fearful of motion. Since they move by night, their eyes are quite large and keen of sight.

along the rocky ledge toward the leopard. Watching the troop, the leopard did not notice the defenders, who dropped on him from above. One bit his spine, the other his throat. The surprised leopard seized the baboon on his back, and with one stroke of his paw tore away the belly of the baboon hanging to his throat. But it was too late, for the baboon's canine teeth had severed the jugular vein. Both defenders died, but so did the invader. On the human side, this incident graphically illustrates John 15:13: "Greater love has no one than this, that one lay down his life for his friends." That's what Jesus did for each of us.

Guide Factory

Facts about... GORILLAS AND MONKEYS

- The largest primates are the lowland gorillas of Africa, which are nearly six feet tall. They may have a 60-inch chest and weigh as much as 360 pounds.

- The smallest monkey is the pygmy marmoset of South America, which weighs only two and one-half ounces. They are squirrel-like, with high-pitched voices. Insects, spiders, and fruit are their main fare. Some pygmy marmosets have ringed tails, similar to the larger ring-tailed femurs.

Chapter Two

In THE DOGHOUSE

CANINES ON THE JOB

Dogs are fun to cuddle and play with. But dogs can also do their share of work. The most common working dogs are those trained to herd cattle. Native Americans regularly used dogs to carry burdens.

For many centuries the sled dog has been truly a work dog. As a rule a sled dog, such as the Eskimo dog, Alaskan malamute, or Siberian husky, can pull twice its own weight. The average husky weighs 50 pounds, the malamute 85, and both can travel at a steady speed of 13 miles per hour. In a sled-dog race from Anchorage to Nome, Alaska, a distance of 1, 049 miles, a team of dogs made the trip in 14 days, 14 hours, and 43 minutes. The longest recorded sled journey was the 3,720-mile trek by the Herbert expedition over the Polar ice.

There are two methods of hitching dogs to a sled: the gang hitch, in which the dogs are paired behind a leader, and the fan hitch, in which all the dogs pull, side-by-side. The second method is safer if crevasses are a danger.

The Eskimo dog has the honor of having pulled sleds to both the North and South poles. Its origin goes back to eastern Siberia. These dogs come in all colors, from white to black, with gray being the most common. They have two kinds of hair—the undercoat, which is soft and woolly and about two inches long, and the outer coat, which is long, coarse, close-set, and weather resistant. The tail, bushy and curled, is used to cover over its face when sleeping on snow. This hardy animal can sleep on or in snow in temperatures of −40° to −50° Fahrenheit. This is evidence of an incredibly efficient body temperature control system. This ability to maintain a constant body temperature, independent of the environment, is known as homoiothermism and is possessed to some degree by all mammals and birds.

The Alaskan malamute, the strongest sled dog, is related to the Eskimo dog. Its name comes from a

"SEEING" WITHOUT EYES

In modern times the working dog of the greatest use is the guide dog. These Seeing Eye dogs are the most highly trained dogs on earth. Many blind persons have gained greater freedom of movement because of guide dogs. One of the hardest lessons they have to learn is to ignore other animals and interesting odors. Most, but not all, guide dogs are female German shepherds.

CATCHING CROOKS

The bloodhound is a large dog that always seems to wear a sad expression. This breed is quite old, having been known in the Mediterranean area before the time of Christ. They were brought to Western Europe during the Crusades because of their value in having a keen sense of smell when on a trail. In spite of its unappealing name, the bloodhound is one of the kindest and gentlest of all breeds; tales of its viciousness are untrue. This dog will follow a trail relentlessly, but unlike the police dog, it does not attack the person being tracked. Nick Carter, a famous bloodhound, started on the four-day-old trail of a criminal and found the man. This particular dog is credited with being responsible for several hundred convictions. Another dog successfully followed a fleeing criminal for 138 miles. A sense of smell that keen seems incredible to us humans, whose noses are comparatively weak.

native Inuit tribe called the Malemiut.

The Siberian husky, small and fast, was imported from Siberia to Alaska in 1909. Another sled dog, the Samoyed, is perhaps the most beautiful of this type. Developed to herd reindeer, it originated in central Russia among the Samoyedic people. It is a much-admired show dog.

THE SAINT BERNARD STORY

Bernard of Menthon, later Saint Bernard, was

born in A. D. 923 near Annecy, France. His father, a duke and a large landowner, sent Bernard to the university at Paris for his education. Some faculty members there were dedicated Christians and tried to bring the message of salvation through Christ to interested students. Young Bernard was among those and accepted Jesus Christ as his Forever Friend. But upon returning home, Bernard discovered that his deep interest in religious things greatly angered his wealthy father. Bernard was locked in his bedroom, and his father declared that he would be fed only bread and water until he came to his senses and was ready to prepare to take over the dukedom. Bernard loved his father and did not wish to displease him, but he was determined to be a servant of God. During the night he made a bundle of his clothes and threw them out the window. Then, tying bedsheets together, he slid down two stories to the ground and took the road toward Aosta in Italy, where he had friends. He was soon out of his father's dukedom.

In Aosta, Bernard joined an Augustinian monastery and trained for the ministry. This city was located at the Italian end of the main road over the Alps, and the young man soon saw the perilous conditions high in the mountains where many travelers lost their lives during fall and winter. With the help of his friends, he built two hospices, or travelers' inns. The larger one was at the Great St. Bernard

Pass; the smaller was located several miles away.

The task of the men and dogs stationed at these inns was to take care of travelers, particularly in stormy weather. These dogs, a cross between the Great Pyrenees and several other breeds, possessed a marvelous sense of direction and a keen sense of smell, making them ideal for rescue work. They could detect a snow-buried victim 900 feet away, and for that reason were also known as avalanche dogs. They also possessed an uncanny ability to anticipate weather changes that could cause snow slides that often buried travelers.

The most famous of all Saint Bernard dogs was Barry, who saved the lives of 40 travelers. His stuffed body stands today in a museum in Bern, Switzerland.

no nose knows like this nose

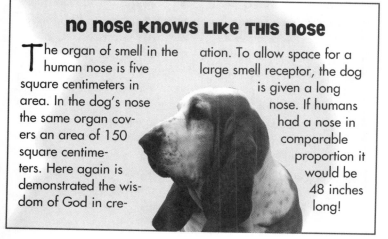

The organ of smell in the human nose is five square centimeters in area. In the dog's nose the same organ covers an area of 150 square centimeters. Here again is demonstrated the wisdom of God in creation. To allow space for a large smell receptor, the dog is given a long nose. If humans had a nose in comparable proportion it would be 48 inches long!

As pets and show dogs, Saint Bernards are still popular, and thoroughbreds have been sold for as much as $6,000.

FAITHFUL UNTO DEATH

One warm day in 1936 the local train pulled slowly out of the station at Fort Benton, Montana. It carried in a casket the body of an old sheepherder being sent to a distant state for burial. There was only one mourner—a half-breed collie named Shep, who for years had been the shepherd's constant companion.

Not understanding the meaning of death, the

FIND THE PROFESSOR

To test the animal's ability to smell, a teacher at the University of Tennessee had his dog kept at home while he and 12 students walked from his back door across a field. The professor headed the column, so his footprints were covered by those of his students. At the end of one mile the group split, six went to the left, and six to the right. The teacher headed the group going to the right. A half mile farther on both groups scattered and the professor hid. His dog was released and told to find him. The animal trailed the group to the division without hesitation, took the trail to the right, reached the scattering point, and had no trouble locating his master. How did the animal do this? By using an acute, God-created, selective sense of smell.

BRAVING THE FLAMES

In the historic Oak Dale Cemetery in Wilmington, North Carolina, is the grave of a dog who broke away from restraining hands and rushed into a flaming home, only to die beside his crippled master, whom he tried vainly to save. Touched by this heroism, Oak Dale permitted dog and master to be buried together, the faithful animal held in the man's arms.

animal knew only that his master had gone away on a train and that he must wait for his return. On that day began a long vigil, for from that time the dog never left the station. He made a home of sorts under the platform, day by day meeting each train, watching for the familiar form to return.

Understanding the reason for Shep's loyal wait, the station master fed and watered him. When winter came, he made a bed for him in the freight house. The news spread, and many people tried to give the dog a home, but he would not give up his self-imposed task. Time went on, and Shep grew stiff and slow and deaf. On January 12, 1942, the old dog was killed by a train as he limped across the tracks. Fort Benton mourned the death and buried him with honor. The dog's body was placed in a black casket, handmade by the station agent, and was carried by the town's Boy Scout troop to a high bluff overlooking the depot. At the grave site the local minister read a eulogy, taps sounded, and Shep was buried. Later, a monument was erected, featuring a dog's resting form.

This is not the end of Shep's influence. Conductor Edward Shields of the local train, who had seen the faithful dog every day for six years, published a booklet about Shep and sold it to his passengers. This earned a profit that Mr. Shields gave to the Montana School for the Deaf and Blind in Great Falls. This "Shep Fund" idea received wide publicity, and gifts poured in to help the school's visually-impaired children and to fund scholarships. Old Shep is dead, but his influence lives on.

Guide Factory
Facts about... DOGS

- Dogs have nonretractable claws, poor sight, keen smell, tails that wag and, except for three barkless breeds, a unique vocal ability to bark.

- The life span of a dog is usually no longer than 15 years. A notable exception was a Labrador retriever named Adjutant, who lived to the age of 27 years, 3 months.

- The rarest of all dogs are the shar-pei, or Chinese fighting dogs.

- The largest dog is the Saint Bernard, which often weighs 180 pounds.

- Greyhounds and whippets, racing dogs, are the fastest canines. They have been clocked at a maximum speed of 43 miles per hour!

- The Irish wolfhound is the tallest dog, while the Newfoundland is the strongest.

Chapter Three

Bad Weather

ever since Noah's Flood, when the global climate was drastically changed, humankind has been dealing with all kinds of weather. It either produces bountiful crops, or ruins them. Weather has affected history in thousands of ways.

The weather defeated Napoleon at the famous battle of Waterloo by heavy rains and deep mud. It destroyed the awesome Spanish Armada fleet that was challenging England. It drove the Pilgrims off course and led them to land in New England rather than in Virginia, where they had intended to settle.

For good or bad, the weather plays an important role in our lives. Tornadoes represent some of the worst (and weirdest) of earth's weather.

TEARING IT UP IN INDIANA

Seldom, if ever, has the violence unleashed by nature been so vividly and thoroughly documented as when a monster tornado struck the Sunnyside-Kingston area of Elkhart, Indiana, on April 11, 1965. The disaster was studied by Lester Glick, professor of

MR. FARRELL'S FLYING SAW

On April 22, 1978, at 5:00 in the afternoon, a tornado approached the community of Ellendale in Cook County, Illinois.

Ernest Farrell, a contractor and builder, had parked his pickup truck in front of his house after a day's work. He carried his toolbox and seven-inch power saw to his shop, a building behind his house. Immediately after supper he went to his shop to work. The sky was dark and ominous, but only a brisk breeze was blowing and no rain was falling.

Once inside the shop, Farrell heard a loud roar and, looking out, he saw the funnel cloud spinning directly toward him. Hurrying to the house, he quickly escorted his family into the basement, the usual safety precaution in tornado country.

Within minutes a horrifying sound of tearing, rending storm winds, like a hundred trucks roaring by, enveloped the Farrells. In 60 seconds it had passed. Emerging from the basement, they found their house undamaged, but only the foundation of the shop remained. The house next door had vanished. Hurrying to the front yard, Mr. Farrell saw that his truck was missing. He found it a block away on the other side of the street. He examined the truck and found that not only was there no damage but, to his utter amazement, the power saw he had been using in the shop a few minutes before *was lying in the bed of the truck!* Closer investigation showed that the power cord had been ripped from the saw.

social sciences at Goshen College, and his students, who served as investigators.

That Palm Sunday began as a lovely spring day. Warm air was moving up from the Gulf of Mexico, and cold air was moving down from Canada. The meeting of those two air masses created a storm front, a condition that breeds storms. During the afternoon several dozen violent tornadoes, whirling at speeds estimated as high as 600 miles per hour, left areas of destruction in Illinois, Indiana, Iowa, Michigan, Ohio, and Wisconsin.

Weather warnings were broadcast throughout the day. At 6:50 p.m. the South Bend, Indiana, bureau put out this bulletin: "Reports of tornadoes and funnel clouds have become so numerous that it is impossible to keep track of them." Minutes later an ominous, writhing, black funnel appeared in the sky eight miles southwest of Kingston Heights. Woodrow Caton, the sheriff of Elkhart County, was directing rescue work at the site of an earlier tornado strike when he heard "an awful roar" and saw "an ugly, tossing, mushroom-shaped cloud." It came straight at him. He had no immediate place of shelter. Suddenly the tornado changed course to the north, heading straight for Sunnyside-Kingston. Probably half the residents knew nothing of the danger, and some who heard the weather warning paid no attention to it.

Dorothy Warner was enjoying television with her

THE "MAGIC" TEASPOON

On an August day in El Dorado, Kansas, a tornado swept through the southwest part of town, leveling a dozen houses, a store, and a service station. As usual in this area of frequent tornadoes, state employees searched through the stricken sections, picking up any worthwhile items left by the storm. These were then taken to the fire station and reclaimed by the owners.

James Barnett, one of the state workers, and his partner were moving slowly along through the rubble when they saw a wooden case of the type in which silverware is usually stored. James picked it up and found it was heavy, apparently full. To open it he had to release two clasps. Inside was a full set of silverware, except for one teaspoon. He shut the box, placed it in the truck, and continued down the street, here and there locating some undamaged items. Two blocks away he spotted a shiny teaspoon. He picked it up and found that it was the teaspoon missing from the set in the box on the truck.

7-year-old grandson when they heard the warning. She assured the boy he was not to worry, but as the sky grew dark and hail rattled on the house, accompanied by a shrieking wind, she went to close the back door—and there loomed the black cloud! The storm instantly ripped the door from its hinges and removed the porch from under her feet. It plucked a steel clothesline pole from the earth, restaking it two feet away, bending it over the prostrate woman. The side of the garage fell on the pole, but the wreckage didn't touch her. Mrs. Warner's grandson, Eldon, rode the crumbling house 35 feet into the street. His grandmother, limping from a serious leg injury and suffering minor bruises, later found him in the hospital.

At the home of Leo Linn there was no warning of danger. At 7:00 p.m. Linn stepped outside and became aware of an eerie hush. Moments later his wife, Dorothy, heard the growing sound of the wind and looked out the window. She saw "a huge wall of

---

OFF THE WALL

A tornado, spawned by a severe thunderstorm, struck Union Park Gardens, a section of Wilmington, Delaware, where apartments were constructed in block formation with no passageway between the units. An alley allowed trash pickup and entrance to garages on both sides at the rear of the units with their small backyards. The tornado chose to touch down in this alley and neatly removed the back walls of 12 apartments in the process. All fences except those of iron were gone. Inside the homes very little was disturbed. Towels hung on racks in kitchens, flowers and pictures were in place. Upstairs in the bedrooms everything seemed normal— shoes under beds, clothing on chair backs, decorations hung squarely on walls, and books and magazines on nightstands as if nothing had happened.

cloud, black as coal." The family hurried to the basement, their ears popping from the sudden decrease in air pressure. Then came the incredible roar and the sound of the house being smashed to pieces. Debris showered on the huddled group and concrete blocks from the foundation toppled into the basement.

When the suffocating roar came to an end, Linn pulled himself upstairs—but there was no upstairs, just a murky-colored sky. He looked in the direction of his neighbors' houses but was greeted by empty space. "It was unbelievable," he recalls. "Everything was gone—trees, houses, streets. Our house was

---

YOU FOUND IT WHERE?

A farmer in Frederick County, Maryland, shared this amazing story about a tornado's erratic behavior: "The former owner [of my home], Amos Atwell, had kept his important papers in an old desk in the part of the house that was destroyed. Two weeks after the storm a man drove into the driveway to see Atwell.

" 'Mr. Atwell,' said the visitor, 'I have something here

that I think you will be very interested in.' He reached into his inside coat pocket and handed Mr. Atwell the deed to his property.

" 'Where did you get this?' Mr. Atwell questioned.

" 'After that bad storm I found it in a rosebush in my front yard.'

" 'Where do you live?'

" 'I live 12 miles north of here, over the Pennsylvania State line.' "

Joe ashley's Turned-around House

On July 21, 1975, a tornado struck St. Joseph, Missouri. Joe Ashley lived in a two-room shack near the Missouri River. He spent much of his time fishing for catfish, but on the day of the storm he decided to walk to the store. It took him about an hour and a half and, while he was there, the storm broke, so he waited until it stopped raining. On the way back home he saw broken limbs on the road and a tree or two uprooted. He also noted that several small streams were flooded. As he approached his house, all seemed well except that he sensed vaguely that something seemed out of place. He opened the front gate and gazed, unbelieving, at the house. Something certainly was out of place: *the back door of his house was now in front!* Stunned, Joe walked around to the back and, sure enough, the front door now faced the back yard! The tornado had turned his home completely around and left it neatly perched on the rock foundation.

rubble. My small truck landed a block away. Up the street, my wife's parents' home had vanished, and they were dead."

John McLain, Jr., a former combat Marine, paced nervously outside his home, peering at the scudding clouds. He particularly watched the sky to the southwest, the usual origin of tornadoes in that area. "I don't like the way it looks," he told his wife, Laura. "I don't like the way it feels." His wife thought he was being melodramatic when he ordered her to take the children to the basement. She scoffed, but John said, "Then I'll carry you all down." When the tornado hit, the house was demolished, but the family was unharmed. After Mrs. McLain came up from the basement and saw the pieces of toys and the shreds of baby clothes dangling from the shattered limb of an oak tree, she broke into tears.

On Greenwood Boulevard a foundry foreman, Roy Whalen, crawled out of his basement, looked around, and thought, *Dear Lord, it's all gone!* He helped a man with a baby toward what had been Main Street. "Then I couldn't find my way back," he recalls. "I've lived here 25 years, but in one minute the neighborhood had changed so much that I couldn't figure out where my house was. All the landmarks were gone."

Bob Vorhees, a barber, was caught in the open with his wife, Viola. As the tornado's winds struck, she threw herself on the ground and clutched the brick pillar that marked the beginning of Greenwood Boulevard. Bob flopped his body over hers and also grasped the pillar. For a few moments he watched "that awful black thing, backed by an orange-red curtain, as if the sky were on fire, and sounding like a thousand diesel engines grinding to a halt." He saw it kick a car into the air and churn a house into splinters. Then he said a prayer, "Help, O Lord!" and lowered his head.

Within a radius of 150 feet of the couple, the

Inside a Tornado

What is a tornado like, close up? Here's an account from William Keller, a Kansas farmer:

"Between 3:00 and 4:00 my family and I were out in the field when I saw in the west an umbrella-shaped cloud. Dangling like great ropes from its greenish-black base were three tornadoes, the central and largest one perilously near and apparently headed for our place.

"We hurried to the cyclone cellar, and I was about to close the door when I turned for another look. The lower end of the funnel-shaped cloud, which had been sweeping the ground, began to rise. I knew we were comparatively safe until it dropped again. In a few seconds the great shaggy end of the funnel was directly overhead. There was a strong gassy odor, and I could scarcely breathe.

"Looking up, I saw right into the heart of the tornado. The circular opening in the center of the funnel, entirely hollow except for what looked like a detached cloud moving up and down, was 50 to 100 feet in diameter and extended upward for at least a half mile. Its walls were rotating clouds. The hole was made brilliantly visible by constant flashes of lightning, which zigzagged from side to side. Small tornadoes were constantly forming and breaking away around the lower rim of the great vortex. They looked like tails as they writhed away, making hissing and screaming sounds.

The tornado cloud was not traveling at great speed. It dipped again after it passed my place and demolished the neighbor's house and barn, whirling the wreckage around and around in the air. Then it zigzagged away across the countryside."

tornado blew away cars, leveled houses, uprooted trees that measured two feet in diameter, shot tea-spoons like arrows into tree trunks, and destroyed the Vorhees' car, home, and barbershop. Across the street, it split the trunk of a large tree, dropped a lamp into the opening, then snapped the tree shut, crushing the lamp as if it were an eggshell. Viola felt "a herd of elephants trample on my back." Then she blacked out. The wind drove nails, stones, and dirt into Bob's flesh. He was lifted into the air, and as the air was sucked out of his lungs, he too blacked out. He returned to consciousness more than 100 feet from Viola. They crawled to each other. Bob's body appeared to have been beaten viciously with a board. Viola was bruised from the waist down. "Everything is gone," she muttered, shivering in the cold rain.

The same tornado hit a station wagon occupied by Junior Herald, his wife, and two sons. Herald had no time to drive out of the tornado's path. He saw a house slowly rise from its foundation and float to-ward him. For a moment the building seemed to hang suspended in space. Then with "the noise of a million bumblebees" it smashed into their vehicle. Herald returned to consciousness, buried hip-deep in dirt. His wife also was embedded in dirt. Their son, Floyd, 17, was staggering around, bleeding from a cut on his forehead.

The Carl Sharkey home was reduced to rubble,

but Mae Sharkey's mink cape was picked up in the swirling vortex and dropped near a farmhouse in Bronson, Michigan, 40 miles away.

The same storm blew a refrigerator through the walls of a house without cracking an egg inside. It made bathtubs disappear, tore all the hair off the tails of cats and gray squirrels, and drove fragile broom straws into baseboards as if the straws were nails. It powdered aspirin without breaking the bottle. It opened a woman's handbag, removed the contents, replaced them with dirt, and snapped the purse shut. The more tragic consequences included 134 homes destroyed and 27 persons killed.

All this tragic destruction brings these words to mind: I will quote from *The Great Controversy*, pages 589, 590: "Satan . . . uses all his power to control the elements as far as God allows. . . . Even now he is at

---

RAIN SHOWERS WILL BE HEAVY

Heavy rainfall usually accompanies fierce storms. When you realize that one tenth of an inch of rain on an acre of land weighs 10 *tons*, you can imagine the immense weight of clouds that often pour down inches of rain in a short period of time. No wonder the patriarch Job was asked the question, "Do you know how the clouds hang poised, those wonders of him who is perfect in knowledge" (Job 37:16)?

work. In accidents and calamities by sea and by land, in great conflagrations [fires], in fierce tornadoes and terrific hailstorms, in tempests, floods, cyclones, tidal waves, and earthquakes, in every place and in a thousand forms, Satan is exercising his power" (*The Great Controversy*, pp. 589, 590).

WEIRD AND WEIRDER

Most of the examples in this section of the weird things that storms do have been selected from the United States Weather Bureau records. There are many instances of straws being driven into trees, and two-by-four pieces of wood being driven into other pieces of timber. In June, 1962, during a tornado in St. Louis, Missouri, a two-by-four was driven through sheet steel five eighths of an inch thick. A spade was forced 6 inches into a tree. In Woodward, Oklahoma, two men opened the back door to look at the storm. They were sucked out of the door and carried 200 feet through the air into the garden, and one of them was wrapped in a clothesline wire. They crawled back to the house to find it gone, except for the floor. The wife and two children of one man were huddled together on a couch, shaken but unhurt. A lamp stood beside the couch, still upright.

In Ponca City, Oklahoma, a tornado picked up a house in which a man and his wife were eating dinner. The outer walls flew off, but the floor remained intact

LIGHTNING ON THE LOOSE!

Lightning often accompanies violent storms. On July 4, 1978, a 16-year-old boy and his 22-year-old sister were visiting in Dade County, Florida. As they walked along a boardwalk in a park, they were struck by lightning. The boy was critically injured when the bolt struck him on the fore-head, ran down his left leg, and jumped to his sister. A park ranger and a nurse administered mouth-to-mouth resuscitation and heart massage to both victims, who eventually recovered. Since the electrical charge usually moves along the surface, both suffered considerable burn injury.

and was let down 200 feet away without injury to the two people. Nearby, a steel railroad bridge was raised from its stone foundation; a car was carried 225 feet and left upright; a horse was blown from a feedlot, carried 1,000 feet, and dropped to its death. A pair of men's pants, lying across the back of a bedroom chair, were snatched up, carried aloft, and dropped 39 miles away. The trousers were returned to the owner because his wallet, which was in the pocket, contained his name, address, and identification card.

On May 1, 1948, in Neosho County, Kansas, a

farmer received $1,400 in payment for the sale of a farm. He put the cash in an extra pair of trousers and left them on his bed. Later in the day a tornado struck, and he and his wife ran to the basement. The house was demolished, and his trousers could not be found. Half a mile away was a limestone cave that had been used as a stable. The storm mysteriously blew several items into this cave. A later search revealed a dead hog, a hand pump, a washing machine—and a pair of trousers with $1,400 in a wallet, which was returned to the owner!

In June, 1936, a tornado developed north of Nettleton, Mississippi, and moved northward. It struck Tupelo, destroying several houses. Then the storm weakened and moved east. After it had dissipated, a man living about 60 miles away found in his yard a photograph of a woman. Using the name and address written on the back, the finder mailed it to the owner. When it arrived back in Tupelo, the owner was in the hospital, suffering from injuries received in the storm. She wrote to the man and thanked him and said that incredible as it seemed, the picture had been stored in a trunk in the attic. The tornado unroofed the house, blew open the trunk, and scattered the contents far and wide. The same storm carried a dresser out of a bedroom and deposited it against a fence 300 feet away, with the mirror on top still unbroken.

In August, 1942, a storm in Fergus Falls, Minnesota, removed the roofs from several houses and carried a trunk from one attic to that of another, three houses away. The same storm split a large tree in the middle and dropped an automobile into the opening.

In Gillespie, Illinois, on March 19, 1948, a mother heard the terrible sound of an approaching tornado.

ocean in the sky

Before Noah's Flood the water that now fills our oceans and is frozen in the polar areas was found in two places. One of these reservoirs was beneath ground level. Genesis 7:11 tells us that when the flood hit, "all the springs of the great deep burst forth." Probably one half of the water causing the Flood was stored in great caverns underground. Many creationists believe that spectacular caverns, such as Luray, Mammoth Cave, and Carlsbad, are entrances to the original fountains of the great deep.

The Bible calls the second source of water in Noah's Flood the "floodgates of the heavens" (NIV). In other words, about half of the earth's water was in the form of moisture suspended in the upper atmosphere. This vapor created what is known as the "greenhouse effect" and provided a wonderful, semitropical climate worldwide, since the earth's heat could not escape into space. Fossils of tropical plants have been found in Antarctica!

A sudden cooling of the upper atmosphere, when combined with the underground waters, would certainly open the "floodgates of the heavens" and wreak havoc on the earth.

She ran to the bedroom and snatched her 3-year-old child from the bed and hid in a closet under the back stairs. After the storm passed, she opened the door to discover that the closet, the stairs, and the wall beside the stairs were all that remained of the whole house.

THE HANGING THAT DIDN'T HAPPEN

In October, 1870, John Childers, a member of a band of desperadoes was terrorizing the Indian Territory west of Fort Smith, Arkansas. Childers had brutally murdered a traveling trader named Rayburn Weddings for no other reason than to steal his horse.

The deputy marshal trailed the criminal to his hangout near Broken Arrow, where he was arrested. Jailed in Van Buren to await trial, Childers and six other prisoners tunneled out under the jail wall and

anyBody Home?

On June 23, 1978, in the town of Farber, Missouri, an early-morning thunderstorm moved in. Lightning struck the home of Lillian Crowe. The point of contact was the doorbell push button outside the front door. The bolt followed the wiring through two rooms and into the kitchen, where the bell was located. At this point the lightning formed a large luminous ball that floated for a few seconds and burned some of the wallpaper off the wall.

escaped to continue their criminal career.

But Childers made a serious mistake when he later rode into Fort Smith and was recognized. He was arrested again, tried on November 11, 1872, and sentenced to hang on August 15, 1873.

On that fateful day Fort Smith was crowded with curious spectators—White, Red, and Black people, young and old, men, women, and children—who had come to witness the first execution on the new gallows. The editor of a local newspaper, the Fort Smith *Chronicle,* estimated that 2,000 persons crowded in to watch.

The deputy marshal and his assistants brought Childers from his jail cell and led him up the 13 steps to the gallows. A marshal read the legal death sentence and asked, "Are there any words you want to say, Childers?" The condemned man spoke for 16 minutes. He confessed his guilt. He said he hoped God would forgive him, although he had been a criminal since his childhood and could not remember all the crimes he had committed.

As he was speaking, black clouds moved across the sky. The rumble of thunder and flashes of lightning became frequent. Then the black cloth hood was pulled over his head. The marshal walked below to spring the trap that would plunge Childers to his death. The signal was given, but at that moment an astounding thing happened. A tremendous thunderclap shook the earth, the fort, and the expectant crowd. Instantly, a blue bolt of lightning forked down from the storm cloud and struck the frame of the gallows, shooting thousands of darting sparks into the sultry air. Simultaneously, the marshal sprang the trap, but it was unnecessary—John Childers was already dead.

At that dramatic moment an ashen-faced woman in the crowd shouted in a hysterical, high-soprano voice, "John Childers' soul is doomed!" Then she fainted away as the storm unleashed a tremendous deluge of water.

Speculation was widespread, and this strange coincidence seemed to keep crime in check for quite a while.

Guide Factory

Facts about... TORNADOES AND LIGHTNING

- On September 4, 1981, a tornado struck Ancona, Italy. It lifted a baby in its carriage 50 feet into the air and set it down safely 300 feet away. The baby slept through the ordeal.[1]

- The word tornado is derived from the Spanish word *tronada,* which means thunderstorm.

- Lightning travels at speeds of 100 to 1,000 miles per second on its way toward earth. It can reach speeds of 87,000 miles per second on the return stroke.[2]

- Ball lightning is believed to be perical-shaped lightning that floats, typically lasting about 5 seconds. The ball is usually about 10 inches in diameter, and is about as bright as a 40-watt bulb.[3]

---

[1] *Reader's Digest Book of Facts* (Pleasantville, NY: The Reader's Digest Association, Inc.), p. 367. Copyright © 1987 by The Reader's Digest Association, Inc., p. 367

[2] *Ibid.*, p. 367.

[3] *Reader's Digest Facts and Fallacies* (Pleasantville, NY: The Reader's Digest Association, Inc.), p. 187. Copyright © 1988 by The Reader's Digest Association, Inc.

Chapter Four

WELCOME TO DISMAL SWAMP

HARK—LET'S BUILD AN ARK!

many years ago the human race became so evil that God decided to put an end to it by a universal flood. He told Noah, "I am going to put an end to all people, for the earth is filled with violence because of them" (Genesis 6:13). But God made a way of escape: "So make yourself an ark of cypress wood." (verse 14).

Why cypress wood? Because cypress (or gopher wood) doesn't decay for hundreds of years. The cypress tree *(Taxodium)* grows best in swamps or moist soil. In the United States it is native from Virginia to Florida. The best remaining stand of this tree is found in Corkscrew Swamp Sanctuary in Collier County, Florida, 70 miles southeast of Lake Okeechobee and 25 miles east of Fort Myers. In 1955 this 6,000-acre sanctuary, owned by the National Audubon Society, was set aside to preserve the cypress trees in their natural habitat and as a bird refuge. Since cypress trees grow in water, it was difficult to get about in it until boardwalks were built on posts. During the construction, which required about five months, the workmen were often standing in water chest-deep.

Cypress trees are unique in that they have what is known as "knees"—large brown ridges about the base, reaching up several feet. Dendrologists (people who study trees) believe that these "knees" supply oxygen to the underwater roots.

These trees attain an average height of 125 feet. Before so many were cut for lumber, some trees lived to be 1,000 years old and reached a height of 150 feet and a diameter of 12 feet. The state of California boasts the 50-foot-tall Monterey cypress with a five-foot circumference. There are also two other species of cypress trees in California.

Sprawling southwest of Norfolk, Virginia, into North Carolina, the Dismal Swamp covers 750 square miles of marshlands. Cypress trees have grown here for millenniums. As they reached maturity and finally died, they fell into the muck and were covered.

LIFESAVING TREES

Only eight survivors stepped out of the ark after the Flood. But they were alive! Later, Jesus, the Saviour of the world, was crucified on a tree (see 1 Peter 2:24). And someday the redeemed will be nourished by the fruit of the tree of life (see Revelation 22:2).

Because of the oily nature of cypress wood, decay is slow, and the trees remain virtually unchanged for centuries. Now lumber cutters are removing the trees, cleaning the soil from the trunks, and sawing them into valuable lumber.

OLDIES BUT GOODIES

How long do trees actually live? One sign at the base of an ancient cypress in Florida states that the tree began growing when David was king of Israel, about 1000 B.C. If true, this tree has been living for about 3,000 years.

One reliable report told of a tree that blew down during a storm. When the annual rings were counted, they totaled 5,600. If this count is true (on rare occasions a tree will show 2 rings for one year of growth) the fallen tree was almost as old as the creation event itself!

Juniper trees in northeast Russia show as many as

KIDS: DON'T DRINK THIS AT HOME (OR ANYWHERE ELSE)!

Turpentine, used by painters, is a product of the pine tree. One old textbook lists a variety of diseases that were supposedly cured or relieved by turpentine. These included intestinal worms, pneumonia, rheumatism, and laryngitis.

WOOD YOU BELIEVE THIS?

During a good growing season one acre of woodland will produce three and one-half tons of wood, plus the new growth of roots, branches, and leaves. To manufacture this amount of wood requires 3,500 tons of water. This vast use of water is typical throughout the plant world. For instance, it requires 900 pounds of water to produce *one pound* of dried alfalfa, and *5,000* pounds of water to produce a pound of wheat. A single corn plant will, during its 100-day growing season, use 50 gallons of water. Gotta drink water to grow healthy and strong!

2,000 annual rings. Bristlecone pine trees near Wheeler Peak in northern California grow slowly as a result of only 12 to 13 inches of rain annually on its soil. Certain ones show 4,000 annual rings. Another discovered in the Snake Range of central Nevada has 4,900 rings. These ring patterns are cross matched with that of the Sierra Nevada giant sequoia, dating back to 1250 B.C.

At least seven dead bristlecone trees have been located and dated back to the year 5110 B.C. on the basis of ring count and carbon-14 dating, give or take 500 years. Living bristlecones show as many as 4,600 rings. And there are 2,000-year-old oak trees in the

DR. Van HeLMonT BRancHes OuT

In the sixteenth century, a Flemish doctor, J. B. Van Helmont, conducted experiments, proving that a tree increases in size by taking substances from the air. He began by carefully weighing a willow, then planting it in a tub of soil. For five years he watered the tree and watched it grow. He then removed the tree, weighed it, and discovered that it had gained 164 pounds, while the soil in the tub weighed the same. He reasoned that since all he had added was water, the tree must have used a source outside the soil. Dr. Van Helmont had discovered *photosynthesis,* the process by which the tree combines moisture with energy from the sun's light and transforms this energy into nutrients and carbon dioxide. The end result is that it puts oxygen into our atmosphere, and we get to breathe!

Hasbruch Forest in Saxony, and 3,000-year-old bo trees in India and Sri Lanka.

WEIRD WOOD

A few miles north of the Panama Canal is a species of tropical cottonwood that has square trunks. Even the annual rings are square!

There's a tree in the heart of Africa known as the silk-cotton tree, or kapok tree. In one form or another, it is also found in Cuba, Jamaica, and Indonesia. What is so weird about this tree? First, giant supports emerge from the trunk about 20 feet up and spread out for yards. At first glance they appear to be large roots reaching out, but they are actually great woody braces pressing against the earth. Growing in areas where violent storms are common, the tree is supported in this unique manner. In Ghana, Africa, this species grows 100 to 150 feet tall.

Another unusual feature of the kapok is that it produces six-inch-long, football-shaped nuts that contain a silky, moisture-resistant fiber that is sometimes used in life preservers and as insulation. The seed in the pod is quite oily and is used in the manufacture of soap.

No list of "weird" trees would be complete without the loblolly pine, which has a peculiar ability indeed. It can groan and squeak! Here's how. When

WHAT'S GROWING ON DOWN THERE?

A large tree will have several miles of roots, mostly very small ones. Check this out: a single rye grass plant was grown in a box containing two cubic feet of dirt. During its growing period of four months, this plant grew 20 inches above ground and developed 51 square feet of visible surface. But beneath the surface it was supported by 37 miles of roots and 600 miles of root hairs.

THE DATING GAME

How can you tell the age of a tree? Right—by looking at the tree's inner rings. Good growth years create wide rings. Years of drought leave narrower ones.

The first person to leave a written record of the use of tree rings for dating was the fifteenth century genius, Leonardo da Vinci. Dendrochronology, or the study of tree rings, became a university subject in 1825.

a loblolly pine is under intense pressure or weighed down, it can fracture or split. Action inside the tree's cells produces a sound. For this reason its lumber is sometimes used as mine props to warn miners when the overburden is shifting. A similar process occurs when you tear a sheet of paper in half quickly or rip a piece of cloth. A sound is produced as the fibers are torn apart.

PLAY BALL!

Rubber trees were originally discovered growing in the forests of the Amazon. They gained greater exposure following the voyages of Columbus. He reported that the Indians played a very interesting game with a ball that bounced. One historian of that time wrote, "The game was played with balls made of the juice of a certain herb which being stricken upon the ground but softly rebounded incredibly into the ayer

[air]." Another writer, Juan de Torquemada, in 1615 wrote how the Indians, after gathering the milk (sap) of a certain tree, brushed it onto their clothing and made waterproof footwear on clay molds shaped like the foot. They allowed it to dry, and then peeled it off. This is probably the first rubberized, waterproof gear. (Ever heard the term "gumshoe"?)

Well, some smart Yankee traders and ship captains took leather shoes of all types with them to South America and had them dipped in hot rubber, thereby waterproofing them. Soon the idea grew that if this rubber, or latex, was brought to New England, it could be used in many ways. By 1830, 160 tons were imported yearly. Two brothers, Martin and Nathaniel Hayward, pioneered in the invention of rubber-working machinery with steam-heated rolls.

can you stump me?

In one Philadelphia home a wooden mantlepiece was made of a single squared log. The annual rings at one end were photographed and compared with a nearby stump of known age. They matched perfectly with the inner series of the stump. Simple subtraction easily dated the wood in the mantlepiece, indicating that the tree had begun to grow in 1580, more than eighty years before the founding of Philadelphia. It also revealed that the mantlepiece had been built into the old house around 1700.

From then on, the use of rubber expanded rapidly.

The supply of rubber from native sources was so uncertain and of such poor quality that great plantations were set out in Africa, Indonesia, India, Indochina, Borneo, and Ceylon. Literally millions of trees were planted in groves, and the collecting of the latex sap was scientifically done. Rubber farming became a million-dollar industry, especially after the automobile was invented and tires began to be made from rubber. Today the use of synthetic rubber far exceeds the use of natural latex.

THE TALE OF A VANISHING TREE

There was a time when every fourth tree in North America was a chestnut. Now few remain, and the

WHAT HAPPENED, MUMMY?

Using tree ring comparisons, a professor determined that the mummy cave dwellings of some Native Americans in the Southwestern United States were built between A.D. 1253 and 1254.

Tree rings also answered the question of why the inhabitants of Chaco Canyon eventually disappeared. The patterns showed there was a disastrous drought that lasted from A. D. 1276 to 1299. The drought was so severe during these 23 years that food crops could not be grown. Without food or water, the Indians were forced to leave their cliff dwellings.

CHEW ON THIS

The sapodilla tree produces chicle, the basic ingredient in chewing gum. This wasn't always the case, however. When the colonists arrived in America, they picked up a habit of chewing spruce tree resins from the Indians. In the early 1800s spruce gum was still gathered and sold in the Colonies. Later, paraffin wax was chewed as gum (yuck). About that time some Yankee traders discovered that the Indians of Central America were chewing the dried gum of the sapodilla tree. The substance had unique characterisitics. When it was dried, it didn't harden, and the warmth of the mouth—not the saliva—softened it. Soon imported chicle, unsweetened and unflavored, took the place of wax. By 1860 gum makers had worked out a formula with added sugar and flavoring. By 1900 chewing gum became a manufactured product, and machines were invented that mixed, rolled, cut, and wrapped the sticks in packages of 5 that sold for one cent each. The formula was 20 percent chicle gum base, 19 percent corn syrup, 60 percent sugar, 1 percent flavoring.

Today chewing gum is a mixture of about 25 substances, with less chicle.

story is a sad one.

The destruction began in the New York City Botanical Gardens. Herman Merkel, a gardener-forester, noticed several dying chestnut trees. The killer was identified as a fungus that had originated in the Orient and was brought to America on Asiatic chestnut seedlings. The blight enters the tree by way

REACH FOR THE SKY

The most massive living thing on earth is a giant sequoia named General Sherman. This skyscraper towers 272 feet into the California sky and is nearly 115 feet around. The tallest trees, however, are the Douglas fir. One specimen in Quinault Lake Park on the Olympic Peninsula in the State of Washington stands 310 feet tall.

The eucalyptus, or blue gum, tree may grow 300 feet tall, and be 25 feet around. The early settlers of Australia reported eucalyptus trees that were 550 feet tall. (This was before sawmills—*buzz, buzz.*)

of any slight wound and works its way into the inner, or cambium, layer of the bark, where it grows rapidly and begins girdling the tree. Why it grows around the tree and not up and down, no one really knows. This disease attacks the vital cambium layer, destroying the tree's sap circulatory system.

How is it spread? The fungus produces two types of spores, or seeds. One is a dry powdery form spread by the wind; the other, a sticky type, that seems almost evilly designed to stick to the feet of tree-frequenting birds. Plant pathologists studying chestnut blight counted 7,000 sticky spores on the feet of *one* woodpecker!

By 1910 chestnut trees were dying in Connecticut and New Jersey. By 1912 the disease had reached eastern Pennsylvania. Alarmed, Congress and State legislatures spent millions of dollars to stem the blight, but in vain. Nothing proved successful, and by 1918 they gave up the fight. All of Eastern America had become a vast graveyard of gaunt, gray, lifeless chestnut trees.

By 1930 the chestnut blight had spread as far west as the Mississippi Valley and as far south as the Carolinas, and 20 years later comparatively few of these trees were left alive.

Replanting with a blight-resistant Chinese variety began in 1950. If you see a thriving chestnut tree somewhere, say "Welcome back!" (Don't expect the tree to reply, although it may wave at you.)

SIMON SAYS, "LET'S MAKE LEATHER!"

The Bible tells us that the apostle Peter once stayed in Joppa with a fellow named Simon, who was a tanner. A tanner was someone who turned animal skins into usable leather. This process included soaking the skins in a solution of water and shredded oak bark, which helped harden the animal hide into leather. Oak bark contains much tannic acid, the active chemical in manufacturing leather.

WHAT ARE YOU EATING?

Red and golden Delicious apples are the most popular. The red Delicious originated in 1872 from a chance seedling on the farm of Jesse Hiatt near Peru, Iowa. Mr. Hiatt had a large orchard of named varieties. The stray seedling could have been a cross of any trees in the orchard, so he cut it down twice, but each time it sprouted again. Finally he decided to see what it would produce. Since it grew near a Yellow Bellflower tree, he supposed that the crop would be somewhat like that apple. In 1882 the tree produced a single apple, shaped like the Bellflower, but it was red rather than yellow. Mr. Hiatt tasted it and liked the flavor. He named it Hawkeye and, when the tree produced a crop, exhibited it at the country fairs in the area, where it went pretty much unnoticed. In 1893 he sent samples to the famous Stark Brothers Nurseries. The president, C. M. Stark, was impressed and named the apple red Delicious. He bought the tree for a sum rumored to be $5,000. By 1942 this apple was the prime favorite on the market.

BUSY BEES

Apple blossoms must be pollinated, and that's the work of bees. An average tree will produce 60,000 blossoms, and each must be pollinated if it is to produce an apple.

The Gravenstein is a Danish apple. It came to America quite early and was grown in Sonoma

SWeeT SUCCeSS WITH aPPLeS

The apple, America's favorite fruit, is not a native of the United States. They were imported by the early settlers and were probably native to Southeastern Europe in the Caucasus Mountain regions. In the third century B.C. seven varieties were listed in old records. Apples were introduced into England by the Roman officials who occupied the country for 350 years.

The colonists brought the best of their apples to the New World. As the westward tide of pioneering swelled, the apple was taken with them. Characters such as John Chapman, commonly known as Johnny Appleseed, spread seeds from cider presses by the bagful. Chapman's seeding was mostly in Ohio and Indiana, but in 1853 apples were introduced into California and, in 1875, to Yakima, Washington, which became the great Western center of apple growing. The first American apple orchard was planted in Massachusetts by William Blaxton on what is now Beacon Hill in Boston, Massachusetts. Later, he planted an orchard in Rhode Island.

As apple orchards multiplied, the fruit was used mainly for cider, not eating. By as early as 1741, apple growing had reached the point that the fruit was being exported to the West Indies and back to England.

---

a WORD FROM OUR SPONSOR . . .

A word aptly spoken is like apples of gold in settings of silver" (Proverbs 25:11).

County, California, in 1820.

The McIntosh, first produced in Ontario, Canada, was named for its discoverer, John McIntosh. In 1796 he found the tiny tree growing in a forest and transplanted it. In 1836 McIntosh's son began producing the trees commercially through grafting. This variety soon spread into the apple growing regions of New York and Vermont. The McIntosh is probably the third most popular American apple.

Guide
FACTORY
Facts about... *TREES*

- On a single hot, summer day a large oak tree will transpire, or give off, to the atmosphere 200 gallons of water.
- Water moves up the trunk of a large tree at a rate of 150 feet per hour!
- Climatologists estimate that on this planet 100,000 cubic miles of water are drawn up into the atmosphere in one year's time. Of this amount about 35 percent falls on the land, while the rest drops back into the ocean.
- Tests conducted by the United States Department of Agriculture indicate sap pressure in an average tree to be 30 pounds per square inch. Watch out!

▓ When one man cut into a grapevine, sap spurted out a distance of two feet!

▓ Tree roots have been known to survive in the ground for 60 years after the tree was gone.

▓ Apple trees are members of the rose family.

I THINK I'LL CALL IT . . .

A Roman official, Appius Claudius Caeca, introduced this fruit from Greece to Rome, giving it his name. From Rome it spread to all Europe. By 1393 it appeared in an ancient cookbook in a recipe for fried apple patties made of apples, nuts, and rice. In the same old book applesauce was spelled *appulmose*.

Chapter Five

BURIED ALIVE IN MONTANA AND OTHER WILD TAILS

WHY CATS DON'T CHASE DOGS

Have you noticed that as a rule cats don't chase dogs? It's usually the other way around. It seems that God has built into animals' genes those things that make a dog act like a dog, a cat like a cat, and a horse like a horse. This is called "natural instinct," something that is incredibly complex and little understood.

The bird that builds a nest never saw one being built or had a single lesson in nest building. Its only nest experience is that it lived in one for a few weeks, then left it. It's possible that the nest pattern may become imprinted in the young bird's brain in the same way it grows attached to its mother. By instinct alone the robin builds the same type of nest that a million of its ancestors have built, following the same pattern probably used by the first robins in Eden.

BURIED ALIVE IN MONTANA

A rancher in central Montana began losing cattle, mostly calves. A ranch hand reported that he had just discovered the half eaten carcass of a calf that had been partly buried near a large pile of rocks at the foot of a butte. The rancher decided to investigate. He rode toward the location with only a .22 caliber rifle, not expecting to encounter any game. He found the remains of the calf and tracked bears to an opening in the rock pile. As he rode around a particularly large boulder, he met a grizzly, face to face! Unwisely, he quickly fired at the animal, hitting it in the shoulder. The wounded bear charged, causing the horse to rear up in fear and throw the rider. The horse then whirled about and ran for

HEY, THAT EGG IS COOL!

While nest building is instinctive, the incubation of eggs seems to be a bit different. A bird sits on eggs, but maybe not for motherly love alone. Body change occurs in the blood supply in the body tissue that comes in contact with the eggs. This causes a rise in the body temperature in that area only. The cooling effect as the excess heat is absorbed by the egg is soothing to the parent bird.

DANGER ALERT!

Young geese still in the egg but nearing hatching time will stop all activity upon hearing the danger cry from the parent. But the unhatched chick does not know that the call is a danger signal. Its reaction is purely instinctive. Even though sea gulls may be hatched in an incubator, they crouch down obediently when they hear an adult gull give the typical danger call.

home just as the grizzly pounced upon the fallen man. The first swipe of the bear's huge paw sent the gun flying. The second swipe struck the rancher on the shoulder and side of the head, knocking him unconscious.

When the rancher regained consciousness, he found himself in darkness and felt dirt on his face. A weight of some kind was holding him down. He struggled to sit up, and as he did so, his head and shoulders broke out into sunlight. That's when the man realized that *he had been buried by the bear!*

Rising from the shallow grave, the stunned rancher examined himself. His neck and ears were caked with dirt and blood from several deep scratches. Turning his head caused severe pain. There was no sign of the bear. Apparently, the animal was not hungry and, thinking the man was dead, had buried him as it had the calf to provide food for another day.

The rancher started walking toward home. He'd gone about a mile and a half when he met two ranch hands who had found the runaway horse and had come to the rescue. Other than several stitches in his face, he was fine.

In thinking over the episode, the rancher realized he had made a serious mistake in shooting a bear with a .22 rifle. He couldn't blame the animal for its attack—the entire episode was routine bear behavior. Experts say that if you are ever attacked by a bear the best defense is to play dead.

WHAT'S THE BUZZ ON BEES?

Insects are incredibly instinctive. A mud mason, or mud dauber, wasp builds a certain type of nest. If a

GIVe me a BReak

The first time a thrush sees a snail, it will pick it up and instinctively smash the shell so it can eat the contents. In the same way, gulls drop clams to break them open. But these bird-brains (sorry!) don't have the intelligence to always select a rock as a target. Instead, they often drop the clams in the sand, certainly an instinctive pattern.

JUST LIKE MOM AND DAD

In the animal world those whose habitats are in areas where winter prevails for five or six months prepare for it by putting on body fat, storing food of many kinds, and preparing dens in which to wait out the long, cold period. Is this the result of experience? No. Adult animals might possibly know about the coming of cold, but the young, recently separated from their parents, make the same preparation.

portion of the nest that's in the process of being built should break off, the insect will repair it numerous times. But if a hole is cut in a part already built, the wasp doesn't know how to repair it.

Sometimes instinctive patterns change over time. Very young bees specialize in feeding larvae. Two weeks later their salivary glands change, making it impossible for them to do that work, so they turn to building the honeycomb. Twenty-five days later their wax-making glands become inactive, and they begin the outdoor life of foraging for honey.

DO ANIMALS KEEP THE TEN COMMANDMENTS?

Well, maybe not always, and not in the same way humans do. But here are some interesting behaviors that encourage us to do our part to keep God's law.

LET'S ALL TAKE A BREAK

Commandment 4: "Remember the Sabbath day to keep it holy." (Exodus 20:8).

Main Idea: Everyone and everything needs rest.

- After a bird has gone to roost for the night, it continues to grind food. Undisturbed rest is so important that God gave the perching birds an automatic toe-locking mechanism that clamps them on the perch during sleep. Even a strong wind will not blow them off.
- Beaver lodges are constructed in the ponds behind these creatures' dams. The lodges provide a place of refuge and allow the family to rest and feed as nature leads them to do. During winter, when the pond is frozen over, the beavers swim under the ice to fetch bark, their natural food, from logs stored nearby. If they feel the need of further oxygen while under the ice, they have the ability to breathe out bubbles of carbon dioxide loaded air, which are trapped under the ice. The surrounding water quickly absorbs the gas, the oxygen is replenished, and the beaver continues breathing, instead of having to return to the lodge and surface to breathe. The winter allows the wood-chopping rodent to have a long period of rest from his labors of the summer.
- Nocturnal (night) hunters such as members of the cat family, martens, weasels, and owls sleep all day, thus getting needed rest. Sometimes animals are wiser than humans, who often try to get in as much activity as possible each day before they drop, exhausted. Ants curl up and sleep whenever they

DRY SHOWER

Birds standing on dry ground will instinctively go through the motion of bathing. Of course, it's only when they're in water or in a rainstorm that this automatic action becomes effective.

feel the need to rest. Bats sleep all day.

✳ Daytime feeders and hunters rest at night, usually from sunset to sunrise. Bovine (cow-like) grazers stow away large quantities of unchewed grass and swallow it into a four-part stomach. This "bale of hay" can be belched up and chewed when the animal is resting. (Hungry, anyone?)

✳ One very interesting type of rest is known as *hibernation*, a state of suspended animation common to many species that sleep through the food-scarce winter. The tiny dormouse is probably the world's greatest hibernator and has been known to remain in this state for five months. Bears, groundhogs, and many insects use this type of rest to stay alive under harsh weather conditions.

✳ In the tropics there is another form of rest, known as *estivation*, in which reptiles, some fish, frogs, turtles, crocodiles, and alligators go into a sloweddown state of (in)activity during long droughts. The creatures dig into mud along bodies of water or in marshes and wait out the drought until abundant water is again available.

✳ Invertebrates, such as protozoans and amoebas, go "comatose" when certain conditions, such as heat, cold, drought, or fouling of the water, endanger them. Amoebas have been known to come out of this state after as long as *40 years!*

Rest is so essential for all mammals that there is a short period in which the heart muscles relax between heartbeats and a time of rest between each breath of air. The Sabbath principle of rest is a basic fact of life in every creature. No wonder that Christ, the Creator, said to the disciples, "Come with me by yourselves to a quiet place and get some rest" (Mark 6:31).

CLEAN YOUR ROOM (WITH A SMILE)
Commandment 5: "Honor your father and your

mother." (Exodus 20:12).

Main Idea: Respect your parents.

✳ If a mother deer sights, smells, or hears danger, she gives a signal, and the fawns instinctively lie down in tall grass or underbrush while the mother faces the threat. They will lie motionless until the all-clear signal is given. If the mother is killed, the young will stay in this position for days until hunger and thirst become strong enough to cancel the instinct to obey.

GO TO YOUR DEN!

A mother bear in the Cincinnati zoo had two cubs. When they were 70 days old, one cub left the den for the first time, following the mother, who drove it gently back. When it attempted to come out a second time, she spanked it sharply. The baby stayed in the den until invited out by its mother seven days later at a time when no people were in front of the cage. Disobedience can mean injury or death.

✳ Among animals disobedience to parents is swiftly punished. Most mammals are extremely respectful to parents and older animals in a group. Rats, who have a bad name universally, have been known to feed elderly rats that cannot feed themselves. Old animals of many species are protected by younger members of the herd.

✳ Elephants, in principle, obey the fifth commandment. When a bull grows too old to keep up with the herd, two young males are "assigned" to stay with him and fend off enemies. When he can no longer stand up, they still guard him and remain with him until death comes.

LIFE IS COOL

Commandment 6: "You shall not murder" (Exodus 20:13).

Main Idea: Respect for life. Among animals this seems to mean, "You shall not kill your own species."

✳ Animals often sense by instinct and by odor that their own kind is not lawful prey. While young rattlesnakes will strike instantly at any other species of reptile, they never strike at their own kind. Young minks nursed by a foster mother cat will try to kill the cat when they are grown. They would never attack their own mother. Wild males of the same species fight over mates, but seldom to the death. In all animal life there is an unwritten but powerful law against killing one's own kind. Cannibalism is rare among the higher animals, though among domesticated creatures, such as chickens, there are cases of this revolting practice.

✳ When Dr. F. Nansen, an arctic explorer, was in trouble because of a severe food shortage, he found that nothing short of starvation would induce a sled dog to eat dog meat, even when it was disguised with other food. It is useless to bait a trap for carnivores with meat of the same species one wishes to catch. Higher animals and birds will not prey upon their own species, rather they will rally to their defense.

YOURS FOR KEEPS

Commandment 7: "You shall not commit adultery" (Exodus 20:14).

Main Idea: Be faithful to your husband or wife. In the animal world the seventh commandment often means, "Have only one mate during one breeding season." However, in many species it means, "You shall have only one mate *until death*." This is known as pair-bonding. Among human beings it is known as monogamy.

✳ Wild geese and wild pigeons have lifelong mates, as do albatrosses, kitti-wakes, penguins, and jackdaws. Bird life specialists state that 90 percent of all birds are monogamous, a figure that puts the human race to shame. As an illustration of fidelity to a mate, a female jackdaw will fight any other jackdaw that attacks her husband.

✳ Beavers and wolves pair-bond for life, a practice adopted by a wide variety of species. Marmosets and moles mate for life. So do gibbons, some whales, parrots, swans, and ravens. Farther down the scale, fishes, such as the cichlids and the butterfly fish, pair-bond for life.

BIRDS IN LOVE

In Philadelphia a bird lover banded a pair of robins that nested in a rosebush in his front yard. Amazingly the same couple returned to the same rosebush, nested, and raised a family for 12 years in a row!

LEAVE MY STUFF ALONE!

Commandment 8: "You shall not steal" (Exodus 20:15).

Main Idea: Don't take what isn't yours. Among animals this appears to mean, "If you produced it, it's yours. If you didn't make it, and you discovered it, it's yours." To an animal, "property" is food or breeding and feeding areas. To gain at least temporary "ownership" of property the male bird posts "no trespassing signs" over a nesting area. He does this by constantly singing around the borders of a chosen site. This lets other birds know that he intends to nest there and that he needs a certain area in which to forage for food.

✳ Mammals show ownership in various ways. Bears will forage over a certain area, leaving claw marks on certain trees, which is, in a way, "fencing in" the property. Other species go to the bathroom on trees or rocks (gross!) to show possession of a feeding range. This is a common practice of skunks, martens, wolves, dogs, foxes, and wolverines.

✳ When squirrels and other rodents find food, usually some kind of nut or seeds, they eat what they want and carry the extra to a hiding place or bury it. The carrying is done in the mouth, which puts that animal's saliva odor on

Hey—I Own This Bone!

The owner of a dogsled team in Alaska had as his lead dog a big, savage creature that was actually seven-eighths wolf. The smallest dog in the team was given a bone, which it buried under a small cedar tree. It then lay down not far away to rest and watch. The lead dog had seen the other dog bury the bone, but it didn't see where the "owner" was lying. Slowly, the lead dog moved toward the site. The smaller dog rushed out and stood guard with bristling back and bared teeth, as if to say, "Only over my dead body do you get that bone. It's mine! I own it!" The large lead dog, fully capable of killing the smaller animal, tucked his tail between his legs and slunk away.

GanGinG uP on THieves

Corvine birds, such as crows and rooks, select sticks and bark from a common area for nest building. Afterward, if another bird tries to steal a piece, the whole flock attacks and punishes the would-be thief. (These same birds will steal eggs from the nest of any other species, but never from the nest of their own kind!)

it. This lasts a long time and acts as an identifier of ownership.

※ Rabbits, buffalo, deer, and some other animals regularly rub against trees or rocks to transfer body odor as a mark of ownership of that feeding range.

※ Wolves, coyotes, and foxes *will* steal from one another. But to get something without working for it is considered theft among animals, and the thief and its family will suffer in the end. The squirrel that doesn't store its own food must starve or steal in winter. If the thief escapes being killed by his honest neighbors, the problem of stealing will spread.

※ When a cabin is built or a tent set up in areas where animals known as pack rats, or trade rats, are found, these critters move in under the floor or in some out-of-the-way pile of rocks. All rats are thieves and will carry off or eat anything they can reach. But pack rats believe in rat-style honesty, and that fair exchange is no robbery. Whenever they take anything, they replace it with some other object. Their idea of fair exchange hardly meets our concept, because they'll carry off knives, forks, spoons, or anything else they can move, and leave in its place a pebble, trash, leaves, or any kind of rubbish. But somewhere in all this, could there be a sense of honesty in the makeup of the pack rat?

IT WAS HERE JUST A MINUTE AGO, HONEST!

In Canada a wolf killed a deer and went to the pack to tell the news. A passing hunter in a canoe saw the carcass and moved it some distance away, covering it with trash and leaves. When the wolf pack came for the feast and found no deer, they promptly turned upon the "liar" and punished him severely.

JUST TELL THE TRUTH, OK?

Commandment 9: "You shall not give false testimony against your neighbor" (Exodus 20:16).

Main Idea: Don't lie or deceive. In God's wild kingdom it reads, "Don't cry 'Danger!' when there is no danger. Don't cry 'Food!' when there is no food."

✽ When a pack of hunting dogs is out on a chase, each searches to locate the track of the prey. When one dog finds it, he barks in a certain way, and the others hasten to join him. Occasionally an overeager young dog mistakenly thinks he has found the trail and gives the signal, calling the pack. The experienced dogs respond and, of course, are disappointed. In future hunts the overeager one may signal all he wishes. The rest of the pack will ignore him.

HOME, SWEET HOME

Commandment 10: "You shall not covet your neighbor's house" (Exodus 20:17).

Main Idea: Be satisfied with what you have. In the wild, one animal may "covet" the den of another. If the original owner does not return, he may have it, but if the owner does come back, the newcomer will move out without a fight.

- Several swallows built mud nests under the eaves of a certain barn and returned to them each year. One spring a pair of bluebirds "coveted" one of the nests and took over. The owners tried in vain to boot out the newcomers. The bluebird inside was safe behind hard mud walls and would not move. So the swallows walled up the entrance of the nest, and the bluebird starved to death.

The main points of the Ten Commandments are all packed into what we call the Golden Rule: "'Love the Lord your God with all your heart and with all your soul and with all your strength and with all your mind'; and, 'Love your neighbor as yourself'" (Luke 10:27).

Since the last part deals with those who live near us, let's see whether the animal world in general abides by this principle:

- Most animal mothers will defend her young to the death. She will also go hungry in order to feed the young.
- Wild goats, deer, buffalo, musk oxen, and similar animals have a unique

Crabs Lend a Hand

Where crabs are plentiful, if one accidentally gets turned on its back and cannot right itself it will be helped back on its feet by several others.

practice. When danger threatens the herd, the entire group of adults will surround the young, with their heads, hoofs, and horns facing the enemy, ready to do battle.

✳ When pelicans are fishing in shallow water, they form themselves in a half circle and beat the water with their wings as they walk toward the shore. This frightens the small fish into a concentrated group that is easily scooped into their baggy bills. Blind pelicans have been fed by other pelicans.

Guide Factory Facts about... ALL KINDS OF CRITTERS

▨ The ostrich egg is the single largest cell found in nature.

▨ It is very unusual for a male to attack a female of the same species.

▨ Just like a human fingerprint, every zebra has its own unique stripe pattern.[1]

▨ Lizards have a thick layer of dead skin cells that acts as a sun screen.[2]

▨ The Atlantic puffin can carry as many as 20 fish in its bill at one time.[3]

---

[1] *React*
[2] *Reader's Digest*
[3] *Ripley's Believe It or Not!*

Chapter Six

PISTILS 'n' THIEVES

DR. WARD'S GROWING IDEA

Problem: How to ship plants across the ocean without having them die during the journey.

Dr. Nathaniel Ward, a busy London doctor, began working on a solution to the dilemma. His hobby was collecting and preserving butterflies. He would put some earth in a glass jar, place a chrysalis (cocoon) on the soil, and cover the jar tightly. Long before the butterfly emerged from the chrysalis, a fern and some grass would grow in the jar without benefit of water!

Dr. Ward began experimenting with glass-enclosed structures and found that most plants can survive in a closed area, the reason being that the moisture given off by the soil and plants keeps the cycle of life going.

To prove his theory, Dr. Ward shipped two cases of plants from England to Sydney, Australia. They arrived in perfect condition. New plants were placed in his shipping containers and returned to England. During the eight months in transit not a drop of water

YOUR WEED SEEDS HAVE ARRIVED

The seeds of the common daisy, a nuisance to many farmers, were in the hay brought along by the early colonists to feed their cattle. This wild-flower (or weed) has spread to all parts of the United States and Canada.

was added, and the plants remained healthy. Dr. Ward had developed the terrarium, a new and successful method of plant transportation.

THE STORY OF TOGO THE MUM THIEF

In A.D. 797 the supreme ruler of Japan, the Mikado, made the chrysanthemum his personal

DASTARDLY DELIGHT

When the colonists arrived from time to time at Jamestown, Virginia, the ships were unloaded and before returning were cleared of all rubbish. In this refuse were the seeds of an Oriental plant introduced into Europe in the Middle Ages by the Gypsies. Jamestown weed, or jimson weed, is a narcotic that was a popular plant in ancient times. It was used by crooks to drug victims long enough to rob them. Jimson possesses the strange property of erasing the memory of events occurring during the time the drug is active. This made identifying the bad guys difficult.

a Dane in Pain

The thistle is the national emblem of Scotland. Here's the strange way this honor came about. During one of their invasions of Scotland, the Danes crept up on a Scottish camp. In the process a barefoot guide, who was leading the attackers, stepped on some thistle and cried out in pain. This warned the Scots, who were able to rout the enemy in a decisive battle.

From the British Isles the thistle was introduced into America, and today it is a common pest from Canada to Georgia and west to the Rocky Mountains. Only one domestic animal, the mule, seems to have a taste for thistles.

emblem. The Mikado decreed that this flower could be grown only in the royal gardens.

Now, it so happened that nearby there lived a romantic young man who, to impress the young woman he hoped to make his bride, was constantly devising some novel scheme as to how he could please her. As he worked away as a maker of jinrikishas, those two-wheeled taxis of the Orient, his fertile mind came up with the idea that if he could only secure a beautiful chrysanthemum for his sweetheart it would please her tremendously. But how?

The grandfather of Togo (according to the story, that was his name—it works, OK?) had been employed as a gardener by the Mikado, and as a child the boy had spent hours playing in the imperial gardens.

So he knew all about the garden and where everything was located. His idea grew bigger and better the more he thought about it as he worked away on jinrikishas.

Togo planned to sneak into the garden on a dark night and remove a few chrysanthemums, which in all probability no one would even miss. He knew the guard dozed most of the night anyway. He would enter by the west gate or, if it were locked, he would climb over the wall. He checked a calendar and chose

---

aTTenTion, PUPILS

Devil's paintbrush, as it is known in the United States, was called hawkweed by the early settlers. They believed that hawks and eagles, who possess keen eyesight, descended to earth to eat this plant. Supposedly, the birds' super vision was a result of eating this foliage.

---

a moonless night on which to accomplish his mission. One problem remained unsolved: how to see the flowers once inside, or how to avoid stumbling over objects in the dark. A lantern was out of the question, of course. But love would find a way.

Togo decided to use an old method. On the evening of his attempt he caught a dozen or so fireflies and tied them together with a strong silk thread. He then fastened them around his ankle, thinking that enough insects would be lit up at any one moment to

POISON-FIGHTING FLUB

Rattlesnake weed, or Poor Robin's plantain, features purple-veined leaves that resemble the markings on certain snakes. At one time this led to the false belief that the juice of this plant was an antidote for snakebite.

illuminate his pathway, and that no watchman would pay any attention to fireflies anyway.

CAUGHT!

Togo easily succeeded in getting into the garden. He found the flowers quickly and was about to escape when he literally walked into the arms of the guard, who was as surprised as Togo. The man had not been dozing after all! Terrified, the trespasser pleaded to be released, but the guard was not to be turned from his

GREEN FOAM

Some plants that are now known as wild flowers were once very domesticated and graced formal gardens. But today many of these specimens can be found beside highways and in some remote wildernesses. Bet, or soapwort, once grown in Colonial gardens, is now common to most of the United States. It is called soapwort because the leaves contain mucin, which produces green suds if crushed and rubbed in a basin of water.

duty. Soon Togo was in the guardhouse awaiting his doom. He could almost see the chopping block and the executioner with the great sword ready to remove his head, for such was the penalty for chrysanthemum thieves.

Then came the investigation. Lying would serve no purpose, so Togo told his story without evasion. It was all written down in the scribe's book and soon

---

TRAPPED BY JACK!

Jack-in-the-pulpit, a spring plant, isn't as innocent as its name sounds. Jack's only congregation is the restless swarms of gnats and flies that come winging in from mushrooms and decaying logs. Many an insect that has made its descent into Jack's blossom tube has ended up struggling in vain to find a way out. Deep inside the tube, the small explorer is covered by pollen dust. The shape of the "prison chamber" prevents the use of wings, and the exhausted insect seeks a way out by crawling. It finally ends up in another chamber, which is just as inescapable. In the process of all this, the weary insect deposits the all-important pollen on the waiting florets, and thus serves the life purpose of the plant.

Of course, the insect doesn't fare too well in all this, as can be seen if you tear open these plants and notice the dead bodies of the hapless bugs that failed to find the exit. It is interesting to note, however, that insects entering a jack-in-the-pulpit that has already been pollinated find no difficulty in getting out—the walls have relaxed, enabling them to fly to freedom.

name THaT FLOWeR

* The name *peony* is from Paeon, who in ancient mythology was the healer, or doctor, of the pagan gods. Why a god should need a doctor is not clear.
* *Hyacinth* is from Hyacinthus, close friend of the pagan god Apollo.
* *Aster* is from the Greek *aster*, or "star," from the shape of its flowers.
* *Campanula* is Latin for "little bell."
* *Chrysanthemum*, the golden flower, is from the Greek *chrysos*, meaning "gold," and *anthemon*, meaning "flower."
* *Daisy* is derived from the Old English *daeges cage*, or "day's eye." This is appropriate because the blossom, with its rays diverging from the center, resembles the sun.
* *Dandelion* is a French adaptation from *dent de lion*, or "tooth of the lion," so named because of the sharp, tooth-like edges of the leaves.
* *Zinnia* comes from professor J. G. Zinn of the University of Gottingen, who gave his name to the flower around 1740.
* The ever-popular geranium plant takes its name from the shape of its seed, which resembles the beak of a crane. *Crane* in Greek is *geranos*.

would be in the Mikado's hands for his verdict. The would-be groom was ushered back to prison.

Now, the Mikado was a stern and severe man, but he too had once been young and romantic. He read the report of the examiner with interest; here was a very clever young man. Perhaps he should live. "H'mmm . . . So he used fireflies to light his way into the garden. Clever, quite clever." Calling a guard, he had Togo brought before him. Assuming his severest manner and with the deepest frown, he questioned the young man. "Don't you know the penalty for stealing the royal flowers?"

So terrified that he could scarcely speak, Togo stammered out his confession as to the why and how of the crime. He ended with a plea for mercy.

The Mikado, knowing that most of his subjects believed he was harsh and cruel, saw a way to show them that he had a heart after all. With this thought in mind, he changed his attitude and questioned Togo in a friendly tone. "So you wish to marry this girl?"

SWEET DECEIT

Sweet potatoes aren't really potatoes at all, but are so named because they grow like the white, or Irish, potato (*Solanum tuberosum*). Sweet potatoes are related to the morning glory family.

"Oh, yes, sir. Very much, sir."

"What is your occupation?"

"I am a maker of jinrikishas, sir."

"Do you have a house for your bride?"

"Oh, yes, it's all ready, sir."

"Togo, I forgive you, and since I too was once young and in love, I have decided to help you. You

TASTY(?) BLAST FROM THE PAST

An Old English cookbook actually contains this recipe that includes salvia, a plant used today in home landscaping: "Take salvia leaves and flowers, mix into beaten eggs, cream, and some flour, and fry in a frying pan for a second course." (We have never tried this recipe, so don't blame us if it tastes awful.) By the way, some ancient writers say that the Jewish seven-branched candlestick was patterned after a species of salvia that grows wild in the eastern Mediterranean area.

will be married in my royal chrysanthemum garden, and I and my court will be among the guests. And, young man, be glad that I am a kind man and did not have your head removed!"

Togo bowed himself out of the Mikado's presence and with wings on his feet hurried to his workshop.

And so it came to pass. Togo's wedding to beautiful Kinuko was the event of the year. Each guest was given a chrysanthemum, and the new Mrs. Togo was

THE FATHER OF MUMS

Around 500 B.C. a Chinese gardener developed chrysanthemums, or mums. His plants produced such exquisite blossoms that after he died his native town changed its name to Chuhsien, or the City of the Chrysanthemum.

WATCH THOSE WEEDS!

Poisonous plants are scattered throughout the plant world. For example, the nightshade family, which includes such beneficial plants as the potato, eggplant, and tomato, contains such harmful plants as belladonna, tobacco, jimson weed, and henbane. The poppy family includes 150 species, most of which are not harmful. But one member produces opium, one of the great curses of humankind. In the beginning all plants undoubtedly contained beneficial chemicals, as 95 percent still do today. But Satan seems to have been successful in introducing changes in a few that are very dangerous to animal life.

Christ is the Great Restorer. He has promised that in the final restoration of this planet, after Satan's punishment has reduced it to a barren waste, He will recreate it as it was in the beginning.

given the right to have these flowers embroidered on her kimono, beginning a custom that continues to this day. In the process of time two children were born to Togo and Kinuko. The first was a boy. His name? What else but Firefly. The second was a girl named Golden Flower, the meaning of the name chrysanthemum.

SOME PRETTY SWELL SMELLS

Flowers, perfume, and incense are often mentioned in the Bible. The New Testament mentions a very expensive perfume: "While [Jesus] was in

mums THaT wave

The Royal Standard flag of Japan is red with a golden, 16-petaled chrysanthemum in the center. (Other flags of Japan include the National, Merchant Flag, and Jack, bearing a red sun on a white field, and the Naval Ensign, which has the sun putting forth 16 rays.)

Bethany, reclining at the table, . . . a woman came with an alabaster jar of very expensive perfume, made of pure nard [spikenard]. She broke the jar and poured the perfume on his head" (Mark 14:3). Just how costly was spikenard? It cost about 300 denarii, a year's wages for a worker in that time.

The three Magi brought sweet-smelling gifts to the infant Jesus, and in the sad but glorious death of

RICH FRaGRance

Jasmine Essence, a perfume, costs $1,000 a pound. To make a small amount requires 9,600 jasmine flowers from France, 480 French roses, 100 Moroccan roses, 1,800 orange blossoms, 75 tuberoses, 20 pounds of orrisroot from Italy, the peelings from 15 oranges, small amounts of sandalwood, cardamon from India, tarragon oil from Spain, tincture of civet, and small amounts of 35 synthetic perfumes. (Mom would like some for Mother's Day, don't you think?)

a memory around His neck

Napoleon Bonaparte's wife, Josephine, loved violets. When she died, Napoleon planted violet-scented mignonette flowers, which he had discovered in Egypt, on her grave. Not long before his defeat and exile, he picked violets from the grave and placed them in a locket that he wore around his neck until his death.

this Jesus, our Redeemer, "Nicodemus brought a mixture of myrrh and aloes, about seventy-five pounds" (John 19:39).

Just what makes a flower's sweet, fragrant smell? A flower petal contains cells that transpire, or give off moisture, and also gland-like cells, similar to our sweat glands, that produce moisture and oil. The petal cells produce what is known as essential oils, or essences, which have a pleasant odor. Perfume makers capture these ingredients and make perfume. (Today many synthetic ingredients are used in perfume.)

Guide
FACTory
Facts about... FLOWERS

▓ *Flower is* an English derivation from the French *fleur*. It comes from the latin *florem*, and beyond that an old Aryan word *bhlo*, which meant that "the wind blows loose the petals as the bud expands, or blooms." *Blossom* comes from the Middle English word *blomen*, which means "to come into full beauty."

▨ *Origanum dictamous,* commonly known as dittany, is also known as the burning bush or gas plant. The white flowers give off a heavy odor. On a calm, warm evening this volatile, oily substance produces a gas that clings about the bush. If a match is lighted close to the plant, a flash of fire is produced.

▨ The Egyptians used large quantities of aromatic gums and spices in embalming the dead.

MELTDOWN!

When Clovis, the first Christian king of France, was baptized in Reims Cathedral on Christmas Day, A.D. 496, perfumed candles were held by the large crowd of people who attended. These, along with the many candles burning near the main altar, caused the temperature to rise to a point where the candles began to soften and bend. In the resulting confusion, several persons fainted.

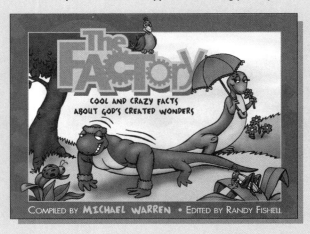